THE VIEW FROM WITHIN

SPIRITUL PATHWAYS TO HAPPINESS

A spiritual renaissance is emerging.
People are paying greater attention to what brings about more happiness,
and what helps us to be more forgiving and kind.
Our spiritual beliefs and practices, although varied, become universal in our desire
to live in a beneficent hopeful world.

Many theologists are pointing to this time in our history as an opportunity
to rise to higher states of being.
Musings of love, compassion, joy, optimism, awe, and gratitude are the voices
of the ancient wisdom keepers that are arising
from the depths of our own longings.

As you turn these pages, you will meet our brothers and sisters around the world
and witness their ways, beliefs, thoughts and practices; all colorful threads
that together form a tapestry of spiritual qualities.
These beliefs are certain pathways to peace and happiness.
They are life affirming convictions of the heart that have stood the test of time.

Copyright @ Donna Martire Miller
Copyright photography @ Joseph Bologna
Edited by Ms. Sandra Rose Martire

ISBN: 978-1-09837-462-4

Authors do not claim to be religious scholars or theologians.
Simply people on their path to understanding that which is cloaked in mystery.
The following are interpretations from readings, interviews and research,
unless otherwise noted.

Published by Green Heart Living Press

THIS BOOK IS DEDICATED TO FAMILY

To our ancestors: The Tuccios, The Martires, The Hrstichs and The Bolognas, immigrants from Italy and Montenegro, who crafted a life for their families, and paved the way for us to succeed.

To our siblings for helping us to remember the specialness of who we can be in this world.

To my children Robert, Marci, Antonina, Charlie, and Alex, and Joseph's children Danielle, Joey, and Andrew. Because of you we know unconditional love. Witnessing you grow and become the incredible people you are fills us with immeasurable joy. To us, the love we feel for all of you is the closest earthly glimpse we have been given of divine love.

To our grandchildren- you have melted our hearts. Because of you we have received a powerful loving bond! Immediately upon first glance we felt the happiness of having you in our life. Pure unconditional love!
To our nieces, nephews and godchildren we hold you as a wondrous gift.
Your stardust will forever shine!

Family has filled us with the riches of love, humor and fascinating memories.
You have given us a fulfilling life worth living.
We are eternally beholden to you.

WHAT PEOPLE ARE SAYING ABOUT THIS BOOK...

"A spiritual life possesses both breadth and depth, like an ocean. And like the ocean that connects nations and continents, a spiritual life connects us to all beings, near and far. In "The View from Within" Donna Martire Miller and Joseph Bologna gracefully and beautifully bring together different spiritual traditions.
Their work connects, inspires, heals" .
Dr. Tal Ben Shahar

"The circumstances of a person's birth ought not limit what she or he can achieve in life. If humankind would only recognize that despite our temporal differences, we all share an immortal soul that has no race, no gender, indeed no cultural identity whatsoever, we can overcome that which creates these biases
and build a more just society."
Ralph M. Martire Executive Director, Center for Tax and Budget Accountability, Arthur Rubloff Endowed Professor of Public Policy at Roosevelt University

"As loneliness and division proliferates our world, focus on myself as a solitary life further increases those feelings. This book, "The View From Within" changes everything! I no longer see myself as an isolated Individual but rather a "Connector", a channel, continually connecting the God of my understanding with all of creation nurtured by hope, gratitude, and love."
Mr. Robert Petreycik

"THE VIEW FROM WITHIN" is a timely contribution to all those who realize the importance and the necessity to recognize and discover the dignity and wholeness of every person. The God-given talents of Donna Martire Miller and Joseph Bologna are insightful, affirming, and supportive to those who continue their life journey with inner, reflective living; thus, helping unite all people in faith".
Sister Terry Martin, CND

"The View From Within" is about love and mercy. " Mercy is when the heart of heavenly love bends down
to meet and alleviate misery. We trust in him."
Father Seraphim Michalenko

"The View from Within" is awesome! Each chapter is a blessing, so many people will be healed. This is a true gift.
Donna and Joseph have given us a glimpse of the love available to us, connecting us to all the world."
Mrs. Karen Bentlage, CEO TkVentures,
President Entrepreneurs Organization of CT.

"This is a beautiful book that explores the many ways that spirituality is achieved. Universally, we all strive for inner peace, to feel love, to have faith. It has heightened my desire to connect with others and share a sense of community,
healing, and understanding."
Mrs. Mary Bologna Carilli

"This is a beautiful book - both beautiful visually and containing reports from many thinkers who have contemplated the mysterious and the divine.
Many thanks to Donna and Joe for bringing this beauty and wisdom into my life.
I hope this book will spread that spirit out into the world. May Joe and Donna continue, as the Buddha said, to "fashion their lives as a garland of beautiful deeds."
Dr. James DiPisa

"The wisdom of this text and the beautiful images will enlighten and remind you that our ever present blissful nature is a choice and accessible. We learn from our teachers, each other, our spiritual family".
Yogi Brian Bodhisattva Buturla OM

⁶WITH A GRATEFUL HEART I ACKNOWLEDGE YOU

In life we meet people who amaze us, who shine brilliantly, who help us to courageously step into our purpose. I absolutely love and appreciate everyone that has walked beside me on the path. These individuals have had a great impact on my life and have inspired this project.

Joseph Bologna - world traveler and photographer extraordinaire, whose love gave this project wings.

Sandra Martire - my sister, wordsmith, and editor who has been an inspiration all of my life.

Ralph Martire - Who shines his brilliance helping the world.

Carol Mancini - my sister who always led our family by example with thoughtfulness and love.

Karen Bentlage - a powerful woman entrepreneur, my altruistic soul sister and my north star.

Ted and Laurie Hollander - selfless and extraordinary leaders who continuously strive to make the world a better place for children and our veterans. I am happy to be a HOMH badass!

Tal Ben-Shahar - Professor, bestselling author, and my mentor.

Megan McDonough, Maria Sirois, Phoebe Atkinson and the team at Wholebeing Institute who shared their love and wisdom. They along with Tal, started the happiness revolution!

Megha Nancy Buttenhiem, My teacher and Chief Joy Officer and creator of Let Your Yoga Dance!

Andrea Cashman - Teacher extraordinaire who taught me how to connect mind, body, and spirit with Yoga and Let Your Yoga Dance.

Jennifer Hanawald - my health coach who keeps me focused, healthy and more resilient.

Donna Wuhr, Sister Terry Martin, and the Sisters of the Congregation of Notre Dame - who are leading me on a beautiful grace- filled faith journey.

Yvrose Romulus - Your inspiration, friendship and angel cards are always with me.

Kate Gloss - You are so kind and helpful, you are always willing to share your talents and many skills selflessly.

Janice Robinson and Diana Piretti Medeiros - my lifelong friends. Thank you for sharing your love and expertise.

Karen and Coach Biebel-Sutera - you held me up with your love and support when I needed it the most. I will never forget your kindness.

Dina Cashman - Your unique talents launched Happily Ever Actions!

Diane Cantarano and Zoe Fox - my heart sisters, The Exchange Club family, Bob Petreycik and Cathy Nickse, Freda Campofiori, and all our friends and family members, thank you for your love.

To every spiritual warrior who contributed to this book,
we are grateful for the time we spent together.
you both inspired us and lifted us up. Your gifts are many.

Clan Mother Shoran White Fawn Piper, of the Paugussett Tribe, Trumbull, CT.

Cassandra Keola, Buddhist, her husband and the matriarch of her family her beautiful mother in law from Laos, currently in West Hartford, CT.

Ola Nosseir, Islamic founder of Our Common Beliefs, Briarcliff Manor, NY.

David Vita, social justice minister Unitarian Universalist Church in Westport, CT.

Stacy and Tom Young, Mormon faith, friends and neighbors currently in Utah.

Swami, Sri Venkateshwara, Hindu temple Bridgewater, NJ.

Rabbi Dan Selsberg from Temple Sholom Bridgewater, NJ.

Jill Levine and Betina Goldberg for your friendship, kindness and generosity.

Father Seraphim Michalenco MIC, The Divine Mercy Shrine, Stockbridge , MA.

Contents

THE VIEW FROM WITHIN

A spiritual life is a
meaningful life. It is
beautifully revealed in all
denominations
without prejudice.

The interconnectedness of
faith and happiness is
researched, and proven to be
undeniable. Whether we are
religious, atheist or agnostic,
the experience of the spirit
awakening in us transcends
the scientific limitations of
space and time. Listen
through the noise, go to the
view from within and you
will not miss the boat!

Mediterranean Sea
Antalya, Turkey

Spiritual Pathways to Happiness

The heart of God is calling out to the world as depicted in these original images and
in the verses that follow. The diversity is compelling. As we strive for an
understanding of this great mystery, ancient wisdom traditions agree, that if we keep
an open mind and listen in stillness, we can experience the panorama of magnificent
ways the divine speaks to all of us in reciprocity. Within each tradition mentioned
here, there is a blessing for the reader. When you read them, we invite you to settle
into the moment, turn the corners of your mouth up just a bit...
and Enjoy!

SPIRITUALITY LEADS TO A MORE SUCCESSFUL AND VIBRANT LIFE.

MAY YOU BE ELEVATED

Every Spiritual tradition across the world agrees on one thing: The power of love.
"Anyone who does not love does not know God, because God is love" 1 John 4:8

1. WHAT ARE YOU IN SEARCH OF?
MORE LOVE? PURPOSE? BELONGING? MEANING?

2. WHERE ARE YOU SPIRITUALLY RIGHT NOW?
WHAT CAN YOU DO IN THIS MOMENT TO CONNECT TO INNER PEACE?

3. GRATITUDE IS THE SWEETNESS IN SPIRITUALITY.
CAN YOU FIND SOMETHINGS YOU ARE GRATEFUL FOR EVERYDAY TO BROADEN AND BUILD YOUR JOY?

Welcome to the journey!

MAY YOU KNOW THE GIVING, LOVING NATURE THE UNIVERSE OFFERS

Today I will offer my love to another.
I smile and so many fears and uncertainties disappear.

In a moment, a sense of wonder connects me to the ancient spiritual teachings of my ancestors.

I can see my future.

Lotus Bridge – Beijing, China

Embraced in nature's
beauty I sense a burst,
a renewal of love
beating in my heart.
In this moment,
heaven touches the
earth.
The water moves
through me.
It carries my desire.
The water around me
carries gentle caresses
and a soothing
embrace.
I am devoted.

The Lotus Pond – Siem Reap, Cambodia

PRESENT ABUNDANCE

MAY YOU KNOW THE GIVING, LOVING NATURE THE UNIVERSE OFFERS

Awe invites love in.
There is a feeling of reverence for that which goes beyond explanation.
Feelings of tenderness and affection flood the senses.
The Spirit awakens.
Grace-filled moments, as we witness unbroken beauty, beckons mesmeric joy.
Love is the path and the goal of existence, wanting nothing in return.

Love's experiences vary. It can be childlike, playful or mature and euphoric.
It manifests in deep contentedness, arousal, romanticism, and in appreciation.
The Universe loves creation with its stars that light up the night sky, the warmth
of the sun by day and all of nature in her beauty.

"The more we know about Nature, The more we know about God."
Thomas Keating

Mysteriously, in a moment of awe, numinosity develops.

Our life is forever changed.

Prayer to the Universe ...by the Millennial Grind

Prayer for surrender...
Universe, I surrender my agenda, timelines and agendas
to you. I trust you will lead me towards solutions for
the highest good for all.

Prayer for releasing of judgement...
Universe, I am ready to surrender my judgement. I welcome
the presence of love to lead me back to truth and grace.

Prayer for shattering limiting beliefs...
Universe, I surrender the false perceptions I have placed
upon myself. I forgive these thoughts and I know that
I am love.

Prayer for letting go of fear...
Universe, I realize, I am out of alignment with my
true nature. Help me see this from the perspective
of love instead.

Prayer for obstacles...
Thank you Universe for helping me to see this obstacle as
an opportunity. I will step back and let you lead the way.

"Moon Glow" Joseph Bologna Images

The Shema Origin: Judaism

Hear, Israel, the Lord is our God, the Lord is One. Blessed be the Name of His glorious kingdom for ever and ever. And you shall love the Lord your God with all your heart and with all your soul and with all your might. And these words that I command you today shall be in your heart. And you shall teach them diligently to your children. And you shall write them on the doorposts of your house and on your gates.

Temple Sholom
Bridgewater, N.J.

Temple Sholom

Bridgewater, N.J.

MAY YOU LIVE THE LIFE DESTINED
FOR YOU, FILLED WITH LOVE AND JOY

Temple Sholom - Bridgewater, N.J.

Be still and know...
I have come to realize that it is not where we come from, but how we behave. I believe in Adonai. I love our Lord and Majesty with all of my heart, my soul, all that I have, all that I am, and with all of my might. I journey through life doing my best to do what is required of me. I practice human kindness, even in chaos it helps to keep life in perspective. I invite all people to join in this heritage. I am grateful for the great fullness of life. I envision a world where we are all connected as one community.
I find meaning and purpose for a life worth living as it is revealed to me in the Torah.

Temple Sholom - Bridgewater, N.J.

MAY YOU LIVE THE LIFE DESTINED FOR YOU, FILLED WITH LOVE AND JOY

The Prophet Moses passed down the laws and traditions in my heritage.
In the Synagogue, the eternal light shines over the Arc of the Covenant that holds
the wisdom that I seek. It lights my way. Family and community are highly valued.
I believe that we all come from the same source. We are all one family.
Let's make it so...

Temple Sholom-
Bridgewater N.J.

"I FIND THAT IT IS WORTHWHILE TO LEARN FROM ALL RELIGIONS
AND WISDOM TRADITIONS... LET US BUILD THE CITY OF GOD...
THE WORLD IS IN NEED OF REPAIRING."
Rabbi Dan Selsburg
LOVE OF NEIGHBOR WILL CONNECT US

JESUS CHRISTIANITY

MAY YOU KNOW MY LOVE AND DIVINE MERCY

"Every soul trusting and believing in my mercy shall obtain it."

May our hands be merciful and filled with good deeds...
May our feet be merciful and run to help a neighbor in need.
The Diary of Saint Faustina

Original Photo-The Divine Mercy

Jezu, ufam Tobie!

From The Collection Of Father Seraphim

The Sacred Heart
Rome, Italy

I have loved you all of your life.
Be still and open your heart. You will feel the eternal love of my sacred heart for you. May your burdens be eased. Turn to me and I will strengthen you. When our hearts are intimately connected, my spirit will shine in you - like a lamp unto all.

"A greater love has no one than this, than to lay down ones life for his friends."
JOHN 15:13 King James Version

The Pieta - Rome, Italy

"If I speak in the tongues of men and angels, but have not love, I have become sounding brass or a tinkling cymbal. And if I have prophecy and know all mysteries and all knowledge, and if I have all faith so as to remove mountains, but have not love, I am nothing. And if I dole out all my goods, and if I deliver my body that I may boast but have not love, nothing I am profited.

Love is patient, love is kind, it is not jealous, love does not boast, it is not inflated. Love is not discourteous, it is not selfish, it is not irritable.

It does not enumerate the evil.

It does not rejoice over the wrong, but rejoices in the truth. It covers all things, it has faith for all things, it hopes in all things, it endures in all things. Love never falls in ruins. Faith, Hope, Love, these three; but the greatest of these is Love."
1 Corinthians 13:1-13

Holy Trinity Statue Budapest, Hungary

MOTHER MARY
The Star of the Sea

MAY YOU HAVE FAITH AND PEACE OF MIND

I am Sweetness and soft tones
of understanding
helping you to untie the knots
of unknowing that are in your
heart. There is no need to
clamor for serenity. Have faith
I will not
desert you, I will bring you
rest.
As holy mother, I will guide you
towards a greater
understanding of the everyday
miracles found in the secrets of
ordinariness. If you trust there
is no need to strive,
have faith.
My son will bestow graces and
I will give encouragement
as you persevere.

The Virgin Mary-Ephesus, Turkey

House Of The Virgin Mary - Ephesus, Turkey

MAY YOU HAVE FAITH AND PEACE OF MIND

Have faith that all the people in the world, especially the children, will help to turn this world around. Creating a world where its foundation is built from the heart. Turning thoughts towards the sun of higher intentions.

The Wishing Wall - Ephesus, Turkey

Message from Mother Mary

QUE SOY ERA IMMACULADA COUNCEPCIOU

"LOVE ALL THOSE WHOM YOU MEET
BECAUSE HE IS LOVE AND IS IN ALL OF
YOU. IF YOU KNEW HOW MUCH I LOVED
YOU, YOU WOULD CRY FOR JOY!"
Mother Mary- Medjugorje

Eglise de Notre Dame de Lourdes - Casablanca, Morocco

All of God's children have many lovely ways.
I delight in their innocence.
I surrendered to a greater call in my life
when I said yes to motherhood.
How beautiful it was to carry the sacred heart of the child
that would love the world in my womb.
I would also learn boundless love as I grew to understand
the tenderness
of nurturing the babe in my arms.
My heart beats with compassion.
I will help anyone who asks for my intercession.
In faith there is hope.

I Love all God's children.
When a helping hand is needed,
you may call upon me.

ISLAM

MAY YOU
KNOW THE
BOUNTY
OF MY
GENEROSITY
AND KNOW
THE JOYS OF
LIVING A
CHARITABLE
LIFE

I wish for all to enter paradise. To do so you must have faith. Complete faith is achieved when you can show love for one another. Bring the balm of love and peace to your neighbor.

Blue Mosque - Istanbul, Turkey

ALLAH created the bee.
The miracle of the bee is
important to understand.
They supply honey for you
to eat and they
perpetuate life.
They embrace diversity.
All the flowers are different
and the bee delights in their
multifariousness.
They are adaptable and live
anywhere – in rock, wood or
hills. For 20 million years
they have been among you
as an example of
Allah's provision.
The angels will come to give
inspiration of his will
for he has created the
heavens and the earth
and all who live there.
Inspired by
Qur'an chapter 16

MAY YOU KNOW THE BOUNTY OF MY GENEROSITY AND KNOW THE JOYS OF LIVING A CHARITABLE LIFE

I believe in Allah the supreme God. I know of 99 praises to glorify and exalt him. He is the true giver of my peace and blessings. His patience is never-ending. God is timeless.

Blue Mosque - Istanbul, Turkey

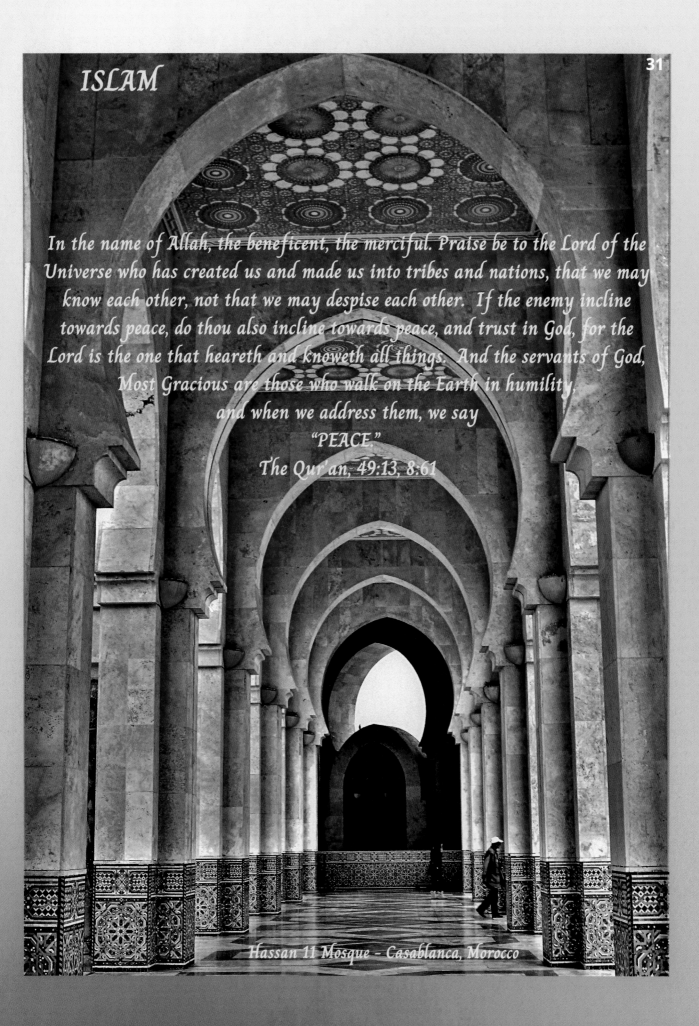

ISLAM

In the name of Allah, the beneficent, the merciful. Praise be to the Lord of the Universe who has created us and made us into tribes and nations, that we may know each other, not that we may despise each other. If the enemy incline towards peace, do thou also incline towards peace, and trust in God, for the Lord is the one that heareth and knoweth all things. And the servants of God, Most Gracious are those who walk on the Earth in humility, and when we address them, we say "PEACE."
The Qur'an, 49:13, 8:61

Hassan 11 Mosque - Casablanca, Morocco

SUFISM

MAY YOU SEE BEAUTY IN ALL CREATION AND MAY IT UPLIFT YOUR HEART

I have a mystical belief that I practice. I seek to find the truth of divine love and wisdom through an intimate experience of God. I take the path of introspection and contemplation. I am filled with joy, as my prayers are expressed in music, dance and poetry. My heart mirrors my spiritual path of love and joy where I experience complete spiritual freedom.

Sikh Musician - Jodhpur, India

"'There's a long table of companionship, set and waiting for us to sit down. What is praised is one, so the praise is one too, many jugs being poured into a huge basin. All religions, all this singing, one song. The differences are just illusion. Sunlight looks slightly different on this wall than it does on that wall and a lot different on this other one, but it is still one light. We have borrowed these clothes, these time-and-space personalities, from a light, and when we praise, we pour them back in."

"My soul is from elsewhere, I'm sure of that, and I intend to end up there."

From : One Altar ,Mevlana Jelaluddin Rumi - 13th century

Whirling
Dervishes
Istanbul, Turkey

MAY YOU HAVE INSPIRATION and OPPORTUNITY TO SHARE YOUR CHARISM

Well being is a journey. I am a traveler in life. I am open to hear the whispers of my spirit calling me into silence, into mindful observations of where I stand. I know I am on sacred ground. My inner voice speaks to me; to commune with the sacred and with all people around the world. In doing so I find that words are not necessary. The universal language is in simple understanding, a smile, and in opportunities to show love, happiness and compassion. The window looking into the future shows renewal as the revivification of my soul begins to transform me. I am appreciating the grandeur of life. The road to true happiness begins here. Negative emotions are replaced with hope. The Divine light of love, nature's rebirth and new possibility is what I see.

Tu Duc Tomb
Hue, Vietnam

I am letting go, finding the path of non-resistance. I sit and open the window to my soul. I pray to open my heart in order to now unblock grace-filled moments. I wish to bring a charitable attitude to what I do. In surrendering, I feel relief.
I am letting peace in.
I am enough.
I've discovered my purpose. Love is my gift to share.

Jagdish Temple
Udaipur, India

Siddhartha Gautama
BUDDHISM

MAY YOU SEE YOUR TRUE NATURE AND BE FREE FROM DELUSIONS OF WORTHLESSNESS

"Fashion your life as a garland of beautiful deeds."
The Buddha

Time will pass by if we fail to acknowledge the present moment. Mindfulness is the gateway into the full dimensionality of being alive. Pause and be aware that you are in this world, but not of this world. Do no Harm. Walk the eight fold path with me.

The Grand Buddha
Wuxi, China

The Jade Buddha - Shanghai, China

I was born into wealth and status. Once I'd witnessed the suffering of others, I was compelled to search for a solution to suffering. I let go of all possessions and comforts to search for spiritual insights, meaning, and purpose. I believe if anything is worth doing, do it with all of your heart. My journey led me to develop The Four Noble Truths. (1) Pain and suffering accompany physical life.
(2) Suffering is caused by desire...be present and want nothing.
(3) To alleviate suffering you must walk the 8 fold path of right livelihood.
(4) Achieve nirvana by staying on this narrow path and releasing selfish cravings.
I do not have desires or needs yet I am not discontent.
I am not deprived. I am grateful. After many spiritual transitions,
I achieved Nirvana, peacefully under the Bodhi tree.

"The mind is everything. What you think you become, what you seek is inside of you."
The Buddha

Buddha – Wuxi, China

MAY YOU SEE YOUR TRUE NATURE
AND BE FREE FROM DELUSIONS OF WORTHLESSNESS

In deep meditation, I am aware, and relaxed. In this state of consciousness my body, mind, and soul are in rhythmic synchronization.
This is inner peace. I am mindful of all that matters. I am love, joy, peace, gratitude and happiness.
I am interconnected with all of life.

Buddhism

Golden Chain

I am a link in Lord Buddha's golden chain of love that stretches around the world.
I must keep my link bright and strong.
I will try to be kind and gentle to every living thing ,and protect all
who are weaker than myself.
I will try to think pure and beautiful thoughts,
to say pure and beautiful words, and to do pure and beautiful deeds,
knowing that on what I do now depends my happiness and misery.
May every link in Lord Buddha's golden chain of love, become bright and strong
and may we all attain perfect peace.
Buddhist Prayers World Healing

Reclining Buddha - Bangkok, Thailand

BODHISATTVA
MAY YOU KNOW COMPASSION, COURAGE AND HUMILITY.

THIS IS THE TIME FOR LOVE. TIME FOR BODHISATTVAS TO LEAD AND TEACH, TO DIRECT COMPASSION TOWARD THOSE IN MISERY AND THOSE THAT MAY CAUSE THE MISERY.
THE BODHISATTVA BELIEVES WE ARE ALL ONE, WE CARRY THE SAME FULL RANGE OF EMOTIONS AND ARE EACH CAPABLE OF GOOD OR EVIL.
WE EMBODY FORGIVENESS. WE HAVE STUDIED WITH THE BUDDHA AND ADOPTED THE PATH OF THE NOBLE TRUTHS TO SHOW COMPASSION, TO FORGIVE WITHOUT JUDGEMENT, TO EDUCATE AND TO LOVE. WE ACHIEVE ENLIGHTENMENT BUT CHOOSE TO STAY RATHER THAN TO TRANSITION.
OUR PATH IS TO SERVE.

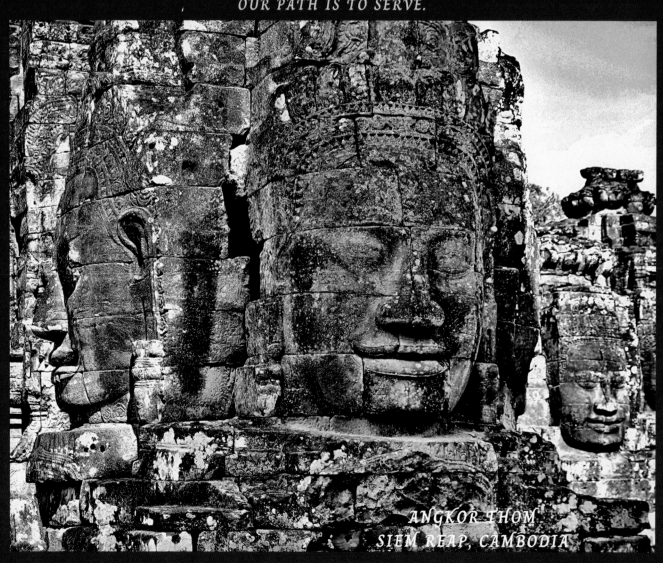

ANGKOR THOM
SIEM REAP, CAMBODIA

MAY YOU KNOW
COMPASSION, COURAGE AND HUMILITY

I am Bodhisattva, I fight ignorance, fear and violence with a thousand arms. My
weapons are all things that create understanding and bring about compassion, mercy,
courage and love. In my hands you will find the beauty of the arts, song, poetry, books,
mantras, flutes string instruments, prayer, chants and all forms of learning
and creativity. In my arms I hold all understanding, with percipience that exudes
compassion and kindness. In my practice I have achieved perfection in generosity,
discipline, endurance, diligence, meditation and wisdom. I am here to awaken
awareness.
Leading all of us to understand, love and cherish one another.

Angkor Thom - Siem Reap, Cambodia

Message from the Bodhisattva

"Extend compassion toward everyone. Those suffering and those that may be responsible for it, for we are collectively as one. The world needs us to reimagine and redefine humanity."
Jack Kornfield

Grand Buddha Complex
Wuxi, China

Buddha Temple Complex Wuxi, China

May I be a guard for those who need protection. A guide for those on the path. A boat, a raft, a bridge for those who wish to cross the flood. May I be a lamp in the darkness, a resting place for the weary. A healing medicine for all who are sick. A vase of plenty, a tree of miracles. And for the boundless multitudes of living beings, may I bring sustenance and awakening. Enduring like the earth and sky until all beings are freed from sorrow and all are awakened.

Bodhisattva Prayer for Humanity. Shantideva

44

Wake up!

You have 1,440 new minutes every day to feel grace and gratitude!

MAY YOU WITNESS MIRACLES TODAY

I rise at dawn; my sense of time altered from sleep. The world is calling. Let me hold on to this vison for every minute is an opportunity to see anew.

"When the dawn from sleep is winging, All the earth of Thee is singing, Of Thee sings the boundless ocean: Praise the Lord of all creations!"
Godzinki

Leaving yesterday, I have learned its lesson. Today will be lived with intention, a first day towards a life worth living.

Playa del Carmen, Mexico

Playa del Carmen, Mexico

MAY YOU WITNESS MIRACLES TODAY

I am present; the colors fill me. I want to take in all that my eyes can process,
turn and share it with everyone. My heart swells with gratitude.
I feel warmed by the shades of lavender and gold.
I sense that there is something else here in this magical moment
besides the blue tide and sky. It dazzles my senses.
I breathe in the miracle of the moment; I am
witness to the world's majesty. I am one
with the creator, the giver.

Playa del Carmen, Mexico

"MAY YOU
WALK IN PEACE
AND BEAUTY."
Chief Big Eagle Piper

Clan Mother Shoran
White Fawn Piper
Paugusset Tribe

Institute for American Indian Studies Washington, CT

In this universe, I am aware that I am part of all things. I walk the path of harmony with nature, the ancestors, the Great Spirit, and my clan. All visions and spiritual beliefs are passed down in stories, dance, ritual drumming. and ceremonies. They are taught to our children in oration. Mother Nature is all ontogenetic sustenance. A vision quest is part of my spiritual journey. It is a right of passage. In the morning dance I give gratitude. In the sweat lodge I receive clarity that I share with my clan. I have a great reverence for my ancestors and believe they, along with the Great Spirit speak to me with every breath I take. My actions are of love and care. Within the clan, hearts are full of gratitude, love, tradition, and pride. Family is our source of great joy.
Together we braid sweetgrass for an abundance of healing, togetherness, love, and peaceful prosperity.
I smudge with sage to clear what no longer serves me and to align with my hearts purest intentions.
We are in agreement. A'HO

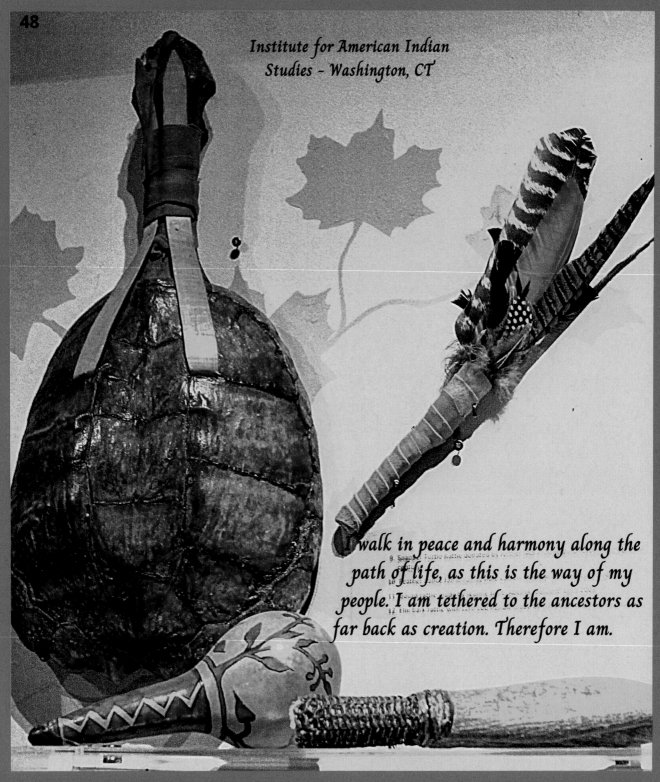

Institute for American Indian
Studies - Washington, CT

I walk in peace and harmony along the
path of life, as this is the way of my
people. I am tethered to the ancestors as
far back as creation. Therefore I am.

SPIRIT CALLED DOWN FROM THE CLOUDS IN A BRIGHT LIGHT. ALL THE
ANIMALS OF THE WATER BEGAN TO LOOK TO HER. SHE SUMMONED THE
TURTLE TO RISE UP FROM THE WATER. HE OBEYED AND CARRID
THE LAND MY PEOPLE INHERITED ON HIS BACK

The Great spirit, that is known by a thousand names, will speak
in dreams that come. This will keep me always on my true path,
one of
love, honor and peace

Spirit in the Sky

Images taken on the Paugusset Reservation - Trumbull, CT

"MAY YOU
WALK IN
PEACE
AND
BEAUTY"
Chief Big Eagle Piper

Sitting Bull Jacket

Institute for American Indian
Studies Washington, CT

"Behold, my friends, the spring is come; the earth has gladly received the embraces of the sun, and we shall soon see the results of their love!
'It is through this mysterious power that we too have our being, and we therefore yield to our neighbors, even to our animal neighbors, the same right as ourselves to inhabit this vast land.' "Healthy feet can feel the very heart of Mother Earth."

Sitting Bull

Barefoot I step out onto the grass wet with morning dew. My eyes close as I ground myself. I am electric. I am connected. I can hear my heart beating in rhythm with the pulse of our mother earth.

Nature is life personified. Spending time and giving mother earth attention will unveil the mystery of life. "Thank you" is all that comes to mind. To be happy is to immerse oneself in nature until we become inseparable. When I am one with nature the world expands and troubles drop by the wayside.

Fortuna, Costa Rica

TAOISM
TAO TE CHING

MAY YOU KNOW LOVE THAT REACHES BEYOND YOUR IMAGINATION AND DEEPENS TO THE FULLEST

My roots are the generations of familial kin that go before me. Just as a tree, I have the grace-filled endurance of infinite belonging.

Imperial City Garden
Hue, Vietnam

Oxford,Connecticut

I meet my spirit in the practice of meditation; I learn to empty myself of overthought. I become tranquil so as not to miss the consequent of my human heritage. I choose to live in the natural world. I am the melody in the breeze and the song that the birds sing. I am in harmony with all forms of life.

Authentically living your purpose is the best way to stay away from the artificial parts of the world.

I will support others with a joyful heart. My posture will be care and delight. I choose my words and actions carefully for they will ripple out into the world like tiny stones causing wavelets in still waters. It is my choice and therefore my responsibility to perform good deeds and to create beauty as my legacy. Virtue flows through me. I practice honor and humility. My purpose is to live the TAO.

MAY YOU KNOW LOVE THAT REACHES BEYOND YOUR IMAGINATION AND DEEPENS TO THE FULLEST

Everything is transitory. Everything is as it should be. Our part is to be grateful.

I am nameless and I am all things. I will see myself in all people and all things. In this way, even when faced with unkindness, I will reside in a state of kindness. "The mystery to this is the doorway to all understanding."
Dr. Wayne Dyer

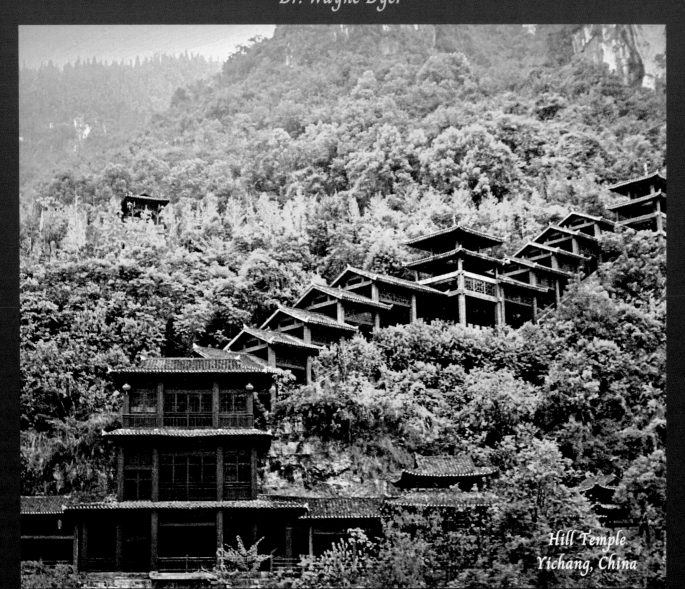

Hill Temple
Yichang, China

Hanging Coffin Cliffs-Yichang,China

"When you are content to be
simply yourself
you wont compare or
compete"
Lao Tzu, Tao Te Ching
"Simplicity, patience,
compassion. These three are
your greatest treasures.
Simple in actions and
thoughts, you return to the
source of being. Patient
with both friends and
enemies, you accord with the
way things are.
Compassionate toward
yourself,
you reconcile all beings in
the world."

"Love
Embracing Tao, you become
embraced. Supple, breathing
gently, you become reborn.
Clearing your vision, you
become clear. Nurturing your
beloved, you become impartial.
Opening your heart, you
become accepted. Accepting the
World, Controlling without
authority,
This is love."
The Tao-Te Ching

HINDUISM

I believe in Brahman the ultimate divine consciousness. He has no shape or form . He is the bond that unites all diversity. He is the creator of all and the supreme, reality.

Angkor Wat
Siem Reap, Cambodia

LORD BRAHMA

*I am wisdom, I have created the four sacred texts that will show you the way.
This is my path and I walk it with my love the Goddess Saraswata.*

4 Holy Vedas, Bhagavad Gita

RIG VEDA- Veda of adoration. Mandalas and meditations on the beauty
 of the universe.
The Rig-Veda is considered the oldest surviving text. It is a collection of beautiful
hymns and verses.
YAJUR VEDA- Rituals from the Book of the Dead, mainly for priests.
The Yajur-Veda's consists of prose mantras and verses. Its purpose was
 that each mantra must accompany an action in sacrificial rites and offerings.
SAMA VEDA- Chants and Songs of praise.
The Sama-Veda is considered the 'Veda of chants' or 'Knowledge of melodies."
 It is metrical in nature.
ARTHARVA VEDA- Incantations, chants and spells used in ancient times.
Atharvaveda Veda contains high class poetry coming from visionary poets.
 It glorifies the curative powers of herbs, waters and mother earth.

58

VISHNU, SUPREME BEING

Vishnu will incarnate 10 times. As peace, as harmony, and as the destruction of evil.

MAY YOU ALWAYS BE SAFE AND LIVE IN PEACEFUL COEXISTENCE

Whenever righteousness wanes and unrighteousness increases I send myself forth. For the protection of good and for the destruction of evil, and for the establishment of righteousness, I come into being age after age.

Bhagavad Gita 4.7 - 8

Siem Reap Cambodia
Angkor Wat

Angkor Thom
SiemReap, Cambodia

LAKSHMI

I am the Goddess married to Vishnu. I assist Vishnu to create, protect and guide the universe. I am enlightened divine energy and spiritually liberated. I am the Goddess of material wealth, affluence, abundance and authority. I am the honorific Sri the Mother Goddess. I will bring you luck and happiness.

"Goddess who is the abode of lotuses, who holds the lotus, whose eyes resemble the petals of a lotus, whose face is a lotus, and who is dear to the Lord who has a lotus navel."
Prayer to Laksmi

I am the Adideva, the Supreme Being that will always triumph over evil. I will preserve all life. I will keep the universe safe at all times.
I restore moral order.
The Goddess Lakshmi, my love, brings good fortune and success
to many efforts of the Gods. Together we are peace loving and abide in joy.
May you always be safe and live in peaceful co-existence.

I am the love and kindness that connects people and promotes compassion
and service to others.
I am the protector of good and will guide you to a meaningful, life.

Angkor Wat - Siem Reap,Cambodia

Lakshmi Statue
Agra, India

LAKSHMI

May you know joy and happiness

I am love in many
beautiful colors, the joy
filled attunement of all
your senses. I am an
invitation to tenderly
open your heart, to see
life's auspicious
merriment.
I utilize sound
judgement.
I will bring you success
and well being.

From splendor to light, I
celebrate with a festival
of lights and transform
the conditions of the
world.

We are Divine femininity - sensual, forgiving, loving and fierce.
We create dance, beauty, music and merriment, joy and celebration.

We are Lakshmi, Sri - Mother Goddess of wealth, fortune, love, beauty, joy and prosperity. Godesses Maya, - I create "Illusions of beauty" with Parvati and Saraswati, together we form the trinity of Hindu goddesses.
Lakshmi is also known as the divine energy Shakti

KRISHNA RADHAGONIPATH
TEMPLE-MUMBAI,INDIA

NAGA

I am a Hindu mythical creature. Considered to be the protector of Vishnu, the Gods and Kings. I am half human and half cobra. I have super human strength. I am dangerous if provoked by evil. I am beneficial to all humans as I am semi-divine. I represent rebirth. I am the Kundalini rising, the profound awakening discovered during meditation.

Angkor Wat Complex - Siem Reap, Cambodia

HINDUISM and JAINISM
Virtues to live by.

- Be honest and live in truth.
- Live in peaceful non-violence.
- Surrender prayer and supplication to God.
- Be non-corrupt and live by right minded behaviors.

"What did you learn and gain from prayer?
He answered, I gained nothing, in fact, I lost anger, depression, jealousy, irritation and insecurity"
Swami Vivekananda

I am Ganesh, I will share wisdom to aid in overcoming obstacles.

Ganesh Statue-Jaipur, India

Jain Temple-Ranakpur India

JAINISM

MAY YOU LIVE IN TRUTH AND NON VIOLENCE

I am part of the cycle of birth, life, death, and rebirth.

Therefore held in me are the 8,700,000 life forms in the world, in which I join my being and take part.

We are all connected. I will protect and preserve nature and all of life. I am here to fulfill destiny by living my highest, truest calling.

In my time here between birth and death, I will let my soul be my guide and live in the enthusiastic, joyful expression of love.

66

I am a living soul.
I will do no harm.
I have no intent to
cause injury, physical,
mental or spiritual
harm to any of life
or nature. Therefore
I am a vegetarian.
Life is precious
to everyone.
Animals, plants
and
humans all have
a living soul.

MAY YOU LIVE IN TRUTH AND NONVIOLENCE

JAIN TEMPLE-
RANAKPUR,INDIA

"FIRST THEY IGNORE YOU, THEN THEY LAUGH AT YOU,
THEN THEY FIGHT YOU, THEN YOU WIN."
"THE BEST WAY TO FIND YOURSELF IS TO LOSE YOURSELF IN
THE SERVICE OF OTHERS."
"YOU MUST BE THE CHANGE YOU WISH TO SEE IN THE WORLD."
"LIVE AS IF YOU WERE TO DIE TOMORROW,
LEARN AS IF YOU WERE TO LIVE FOREVER."

WHEREVER I MAY TURN MY HEAD, THERE
I SEE THE FACE OF GOD.

MAHATMA GANDHI LIVED BY JAIN IDEALS.
HE IS AN EXAMPLE OF AHIMSA.
PEACE, LOVE AND DO NO HARM
ARE THE FOUNDATIONS OF THE
WAY OF LIFE IN JAINISM.
"IN A GENTLE WAY YOU CAN SHAKE THE WORLD."
GANDHI

MUMBAI, INDIA

JAIN TEMPLE
RANAKPUR, INDIA

MAY YOU BE HEALTHY AND STRONG.

The path begins ahead. I stop
and look about. Here is a clear
standpoint. I am grounding.
I breathe in the musty scent
of the earth. I touch the
different textures. My thoughts
turn to time, how I use it.
I think about the decades it took
for these trees to grow so tall.
Nature keeps perfect time.
It revitalizes itself with the turn
of the seasons.
The spirit dwelling in me yearns
for revitalization. With faith
I follow the path.
As I walk I feel my mind, body
and spirit aligning with
my heart. This begins
to fill the hollow.
I feel the nurturing balm of love,
compassion and hope.
I am walking humbly with all
that is sacred.

Shelton, Connecticut

The beauty I see speaks to me of sacred sublime magnificence. As I climb to new heights my body feels strong and exhilarated.
What Divine joy.
I am opening to a holy presence. I am seeing creation in all of its miraculous grandeur.

Monterosso, Italy

MAY YOU FIND YOUR PATH AND TAKE EACH STEP WITH JOY AND GRATITUDE

The sweetest fragrance of the fallen flowers line my path. My soul is rousing. Everything holds such captivating beauty. I feel the sun's embrace warming me. My body and soul connect to this undeniable knowing. I want to dance. Heaven has revealed itself to me in earthly splendor.

Tokyo, Japan

MAY THE LIGHT OF THE DIVINE HEART RESIDE IN ALL OF US UNITING US IN LOVE

EACH PERSON IS IMPORTANT
BE KIND IN ALL YOU DO
WE'RE FREE TO LEARN TOGETHER
WE SEARCH FOR WHAT IS TRUE
ALL PEOPLE NEED A VOICE
BUILD A FAIR·PEACEFUL WORLD
WE CARE FOR EARTH'S
LIFE BOAT

*Unitarian Church
Westport, CT*

*I live in service of my fellow man. I believe in social justice.
My mission is to embrace all diversity and include all people.
Especially those living in the margins of society.*

UNITARIAN UNIVERSALIST COVENANT OF RIGHT RELATIONS

Strive to create a safe place where all can express themselves freely.

Speak honestly, mindful of the feelings of others.

Listen with respect and consideration.

Respect confidentiality and refrain from gossip.

Accept personal responsibility for our words and actions.

Display faith and trust in others.

Honor differences of opinion and viewpoints.

Stay engaged in order to work through differences.

Uphold group decisions regardless of personal positions.

Graciously seek peace and genuine reconciliation.

Encourage the personal and spiritual growth of others.

Honor and support the mission of the unity congregation.

The beams of this church represent the hands of all faiths, uniting in one spirit.

Unitarian Church, Westport, CT

UNITARIAN UNIVERSALISTS

Blessed are they that mourn: for they shall be comforted.
Blessed are the meek: for they shall inherit the earth.
Blessed are they which do hunger and thirst after righteousness:
for they shall be filled.
Blessed are the merciful: for they shall obtain mercy.
Blessed are the pure in heart: for they shall see God.
Blessed are the peacemakers: for they shall be called the children of God.
Blessed are they which are persecuted for righteousness' sake:
for theirs is the kingdom of heaven.
Matthew 5:3-10

Playa del Carmen, Mexico

The goal of world community is peace, liberty and justice for all.

MORMON

MAY WE ALL BUILD COMMUNITY AND EMBRACE EACH OTHER AS FAMILY

"When it's within our power to give love, we should never withhold it."
Mary Ellen Edmunds,
Love is a Verb

Counsel with the Lord in all thy doings, and he will direct thee for good" (Alma 37:37). Prayer is a perfect vehicle for seeking guidance.

THE CHURCH OF JESUS CHRIST
OF LATTER-DAY SAINTS

HARTFORD CONNECTICUT TEMPLE

I joyfully travel all over the world as a missionary. In spiritual commitment
I respect the dignity of all people. I long to unite with others in God's irrefutable
love. I wish to share the message of his plan as a pathway to happiness.
My soul finds its joy in the Creator.
Be still my heart, for I love you so.
I trust Jesus Christ will forever lead my steps.

Stained Glass Mural–Eglise de Notre Dame de Lourdes – Casablanca, Morocco

MAY WE ALL BUILD COMMUNITY AND EMBRACE EACH OTHER AS FAMILY

I believe that the family unit is eternal and will exist beyond mortal life. I grow in my faith and look forward to beginning a family. It is my sacred duty to raise the children in love, right living and service to others. Our home is warm and open to relatives, friends and neighbors.

In this way I am filled with great joy and happiness. I believe in love, light and the truth of the gospel.

Courtesy Photo-The Young Family-Utah

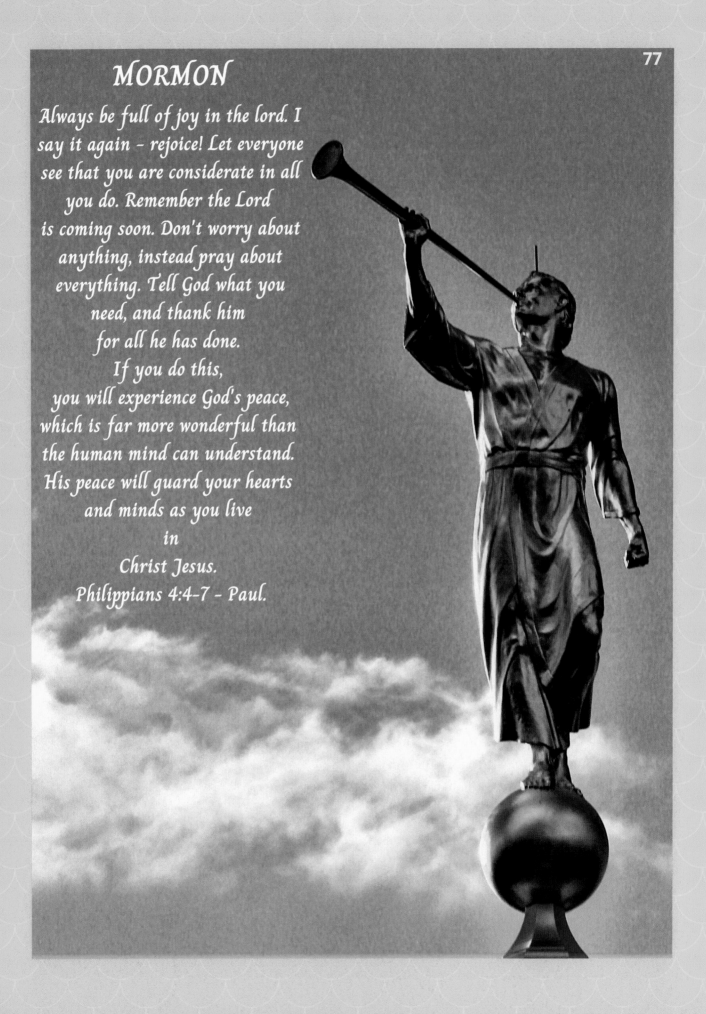

MORMON

Always be full of joy in the lord. I say it again - rejoice! Let everyone see that you are considerate in all you do. Remember the Lord is coming soon. Don't worry about anything, instead pray about everything. Tell God what you need, and thank him for all he has done.
If you do this, you will experience God's peace, which is far more wonderful than the human mind can understand. His peace will guard your hearts and minds as you live in Christ Jesus.
Philippians 4:4-7 - Paul.

SHINTOISM
MAY YOU BE MINDFUL AND FULFILL YOUR DESTINY.

Shinto means "the way of the Gods".
I meet my ancestral Kami on the trail of life. Their spirits are in the wind, the trees, the mountains, and the rivers.
All of nature is Kami and is sacred.
Here my heart and my mind are at peace.
I have an affinity with natural beauty for it's harmony with spirits.
I purify myself in the cleansing waters.
The divine is all around - confirmed in the power of the living, restorative natural environment that surrounds us.

Fushimi Inari Shinto Shrine-Kyoto, Japan

PASS THROUGH THE GATES THAT WILL LEAD YOU TO YOUR HEAVENLY HOME

A torii is a traditional Japanese gate most commonly found at the entrance of or within a Shinto shrine where it symbolically marks the transition from the mundane to the sacred.

Fushimi Inari Shinto Shrine - Kyoto, Japan

Kasugataisha Shrine–Nara,Japan

I visit the shrines of the ancestors. As I enter the gates, the lanterns light the way and show a distinct line between this life and the next. Each lantern holds a spirit Kami for guidance. The more gates one passes the holier the area. This is sacred ground. I bow in respect for the ancestors and the Kami at every gate,

I have a heart of truth.
I am honest and loyal.
I live a good life.
The shrines we build are
to lead the Kami,
the ancestors to their
heavenly place
of honor.
I value purity.
Water cleanses my mind,
heart and soul.
My actions are in truth,
gratitude and
right living.

Fushimi Inari Shrine - Kyoto, Japan

Fushimi Inari Shinto Shrine - Kyoto, Japan

MAY YOU BE MINDFUL AND FULFILL YOUR DESTINY.

SHINTO

1. There is no founder, dogma or official scriptures.
2. Kami are present in all things and nature is at the center of the beliefs.
3. Everything intelligent is considered Kami.
4. Japanese Emperors, considered the descendants of the Sun God, performed the first rituals.

Jinja - Honcho association of Shinto Shrines.

Fushimi Inari Shrine-Kyoto, Japan

YOGA
MAY YOU FIND A PATH TO HEALTH AND HAPPINESS

YOGA IS A METHOD OF PHYSICAL, MENTAL AND SPIRITUAL PRACTICES WHICH ORIGINATED IN ANCIENT INDIA. TODAY, IT IS THE PRACTICE OF NON-COMPETITIVE PHYSICAL EXERCISE.
IT PLAYS A VITAL ROLE IN HEALTH, WELL-BEING, AND IMPROVING FLEXIBILITY. IT IMPACTS THE PARASYMPATHETIC NERVOUS SYSTEM IMPROVING THE ABILITY TO REST, DIGEST, BREATHE DEEPLY, STAY CALM AND LOWER BLOOD PRESSURE. YOGA IS KNOWN TO IMPROVE HEART HEALTH. WITH CONTINUED PRACTICE, IT PROVIDES ALTERNATE PATHS TO UNION WITH GOD.

WAT PO
BANGKOK, THAILAND

YOGIC, MORAL BEHAVIORS

YAMAS

Ahimsa - Non-Violence, Freedom from Harming anyone or anything.

Satya- Truthfulness, live authentically, be honest with yourself and others.

Asteya - Non-Stealing, Freedom from Stealing. Non attachment from material
things. Refrain from coveting.

Brahmacharya- Moderation in everything. There is no need for waste
or excess.

Aparigraha - Non-Hoarding, Freedom from Grasping. Live without
the trappings of lust or greed.

NIYAMAS

Saucha - Cleanliness, purity of mind and body.

Santosha - Contentment, being grateful for what one has, finding balance.

Tapas - Self-Discipline, light the fire inside of you to rid yourself of impurities
and unhealthy cravings.

Svadhyaya - Self-Study, Study through introspection and read scriptures
from the Masters.

Isvara - Pranidhana Surrender to the supreme being. Be an instrument
of God's peace.

Milford, Connecticut

YOGA
MAY YOU FIND A PATH
TO HEALTH AND
HAPPINESS

I recognize Divinity
in everything. I delight
in knowing the Divine presence
is in me and I see the face
of God in you. My yoga
is unity with the source. When
I practice, my thoughts, words,
actions and emotions are
in harmony. I find serenity
in meditation. I find joy
in chanting and dancing
through the Chakras. I study
the eight limbs of my practice.
In mind, body and spirit
I practice right livelihood.
In service to community
and others, my love grows
and remains uninterrupted.

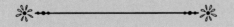

Wat Po
Bangkok, Thailand

YOGA - Patanjali's Eight fold Path.

1. Integrity and ethical standards.
   "Do unto others as you would have done to you."
2. Self regulation. Attend Spiritual Observances.
3. Master the Postures practiced in yoga.
   They develop the ability to concentrate and one will begin to value the body as a temple of the spirit.
4. Master "The breath", it is the life force extension.

.5. Sensory transcendence. The ability to look at ourselves and observe habits that interfere with internal growth.
6. Slow down the thinking practice by focusing on one thing.
7. Meditation. Entering the silence. The Spiritual dwelling place inside us.
8. Interconnectedness to all things. Enlightenment.

Ranthambore Park-
Rajasthan,India

life is beautiful and wondrous.

UBUNTU - AFRICAN HUMANISM

I am because you are. Therefore, I shall extend the same kindness to you as I would hope to have extended to me.

Maasai Mara
Kenya, Africa

Maasai Children Kenya

THE COMMUNITY TEACHES US IN SONGS AND FABLES.
WE DEPEND ON EACH OTHER TO BE KIND AND LOVING.
I AM A DIGNIFIED PERSON
BECAUSE YOU ARE TOO.

Children of the Maasi Tribe

May we all join in our common humanity with kindness.

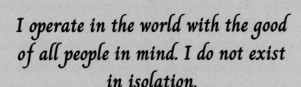

I operate in the world with the good
of all people in mind. I do not exist
in isolation.
I believe that every thought I have
and everything I do affects t
he whole world.
I will show empathy because
you and I
are on the same path together. I will not
compete with you or leave you behind.
I will treat you with love and kindness
always, for you and I are the same
person.

UBUNTU

The essence of being a person. We are people through other people. We can not be fully human alone. We are made for interdependence, we are made for family. When you have UBUNTU, you embrace others. You are generous and compassionate.

"IF the world had ubuntu, we would not have war. We would not have the gaps between the rich and the poor. You are rich so that you can make up what is lacking for others. You are powerful to help the weak. Just as a mother or father helps their children.
This is Gods dream!"

Desmond Tutu

Masaai Mara Plateau Kenya, Africa

A heart full of love needs
no words to express itself.
In the eyes of this beholder,
behind a camera,
it is bittersweet. What
a journey. Take good care
kind sir.
Our paths may never cross again
but I am grateful for this
exchange, one man to another.
We are strangers in most ways,
yet you extend your wave
in a moment of kindness. I will
never forget how warm
and accepting
that made me feel.
Our beliefs, our prayers, our
mantras, rituals, traditions,
solemnities, ceremonies,
ordinances, sacraments, habits
and practices lead us to one
thing... The recognition of
the Divine nature we all possess.
The spirit of love is alive in each
and every one of us. Thank you
for that exchange.
Peace.

The Wave~
Jodhpur, India

"SOMEDAY AFTER MASTERING THE WINDS, THE WATER AND GRAVITY, WE SHALL HARNESS FOR GOD THE ENERGY OF LOVE, AND THEN FOR THE SECOND TIME IN HISTORY, WE WILL HAVE DISCOVERED FIRE"
PIERRE TEILHARD DE CHARDIN

IN THIS RESEARCH AND IN THE MANY INSIGHTFUL CONVERSATIONS MADE ON THE BEHALF OF THIS BOOK, WE FOUND THAT THESE MYSTICAL TRUTHS ECHOED ACROSS THEM ALL.

- SILENCE....THAT IN WHICH WE SEARCH FOR IS FOUND IN SILENCE, AS WE GO INTO OUR OWN CONTEMPLATIVE INDWELLING PLACE IN PRAYER, MEDITATION, CHANTING, OR MOVEMENT.

- AWE...THE SURPRISING EMOTIONAL AROUSAL WHEN YOU EXPERIENCE A MOMENT OF AMAZEMENT, BEAUTY, OR MAGNIFICENCE.

- FORGIVENESS... IS A CERTAIN PATHWAY TO INCREASE LOVE AND TENDERNESS.

- COMPASSION... ALLOWS US TO SEE OURSELVES IN OTHERS AND TO EXPRESS KINDNESS.

- UNITY...REVERENCE FOR ALL LIFE.

- GRATITUDE... IS GRACE.

- GOODNESS... SPEAK, BEHAVE AND LIVE RIGHT-MINDED.

- BELONGING...WE ARE ALL BORN OF THE SAME SOURCE. WE ALL MATTER.

- SERVICE... TAKE ACTION, LOVE, AND CARE FOR OTHERS. SHARE YOUR GIFTS

- LOVE... IS THE GIVER OF ALL THINGS. LOVE IS THE DIVINE. THE GREATEST OF ALL THESE THINGS IS LOVE.

Gratitude is an important part of the spiritual journey.

"Grateful living brings in place of greed: sharing;
in place of oppression: respect;
in place of violence: peace. "
"Who does not long for a world of sharing, mutual respect, and peace?"

BROTHER DAVID STENDLE RAST

Gratitude is an intention, an attitude that aligns us with our values and our truths. Recognizing the beauty in nature, the love of our neighbor, the ability to give charitably to another, are some of the golden threads that connect us to gratitude and increased happiness. In this way our prayers, chants, songs and meditations are simply this... Thank you...

A grateful heart is hopeful and optimistic, it is faithful. Gratitude enhances spiritual growth. We develop the habit of counting our blessings and noticing the good in our life. It refocuses us on what really matters. We become filled with grace as we focus on what we have instead of what we lack. Gratitude is one of the higher human character strengths. It builds resiliency, our ability to cope. Gratitude helps people feel more positive emotions, relish good experiences, improve their health, deal with adversity, and build strong relationships.

We can get up every day and say today is a new day, thank you for my breath, for my smile, for the blue sky, for the love I can share, for any charitable opportunities.

To whom are we expressing our gratitude to?

The Universe, The source, The Great Spirit, Allah, Lord Jesus, Christ, Buddha, Krishna, Brahma, Vishnu, The giver, The creator, The source of all kindness, The source of forgiveness, The source of life, The protector, The comforter, Yahweh, The King, Our Ancestors - Kami...There are many more names for this source whom we search to understand and whom we love...

Thank you God... for everything that sustains us and the absolute beauty in our diversity... Thank you...

THE VIEW FROM WITHIN

The main idea of contemplative prayer, meditation, and mindfulness is to be present, and aware of the here and now. In meditation and prayer we open space within ourselves to feel the fullness of the life source that is always indwelling whether we recognize it as such or not is our choice.
Below are brief instructions on starting to develop a practice to see -
The View From Within.

First find a quiet space. Make sure there is nothing to disturb you before you start. Turn phones etc. off or on silent as well.

Sit in a comfortable upright position on top of a cushion, pillow or blanket, on the floor or in a chair. Invite yourself to gently close your eyes and relax. Start at your toes and focus on moving your attention upward on your body until you reach your scalp, consciously relaxing yourself muscle group by muscle group. Soften the muscles around your eyes and in your face, then begin to focus on your breath, feel the air coming in your nostrils and out.
Let thoughts or sounds that may distract you come and go. If your mind wanders, gently bring your attention back to your breathing. Learning how to bring focus back to your breath is an important part of the meditation process.

Meditating , mindfulness or contemplative prayer are powerful ways to connect your inner self to all that is sacred. Ironically the answers we seek are known to be found in this silence. We can clear out the clutter in our thoughts and learn what really matters to us individually. We are all created differently, not one finger print is the same. Our personalities and talents and character strengths give us opportunities to approach life with choice, meaning and purpose. Consider
all the possibilities realized when we look from
"The View From Within"

GOLDEN HILL RESERVATION
PAUGUSSETT INDIANS
ESTABLISHED 1659
OLDEST CONTINUING RESERVATION
IN CONNECTICUT

CHURCH OF
SAINT MARY
FOUNDED 1832
DOMINICAN FRIARS

BE APOSTLES OF DIVINE MERCY
UNDER THE MATERNAL AND LOVING
GUIDANCE OF MARY.

Pope John Paul II
to the Marians on June 22, 1993

The human spirit seeks the light and looks for ways to express itself in the higher emotions of love, peace and compassion.

By acquainting ourselves with the mysteries of the sacred, combined with a deep understanding of who we are and the world in which we live, we can begin to live a purposeful life and to discover our own pathways to greater life satisfaction and happiness.

Often our search for life's meaning is fueled by events, developmental transitions or rites of passage. The essence of our living compels us to pursue the reason we are here, and to seek understanding of our true value in life.
This quest can lead to spiritual awareness and benevolence in action.

Spirituality is directly correlated with our personal growth and provides a vehicle for reaching our greatest potential. It is the answer to many of our life's longings for forgiveness, gratitude, hope, optimism, connection, love and happiness.

If we allow ourselves to experience the wonderment of spirituality,
the awe that we can live in goes beyond explanation. Shown in this book are
some of the varied voices divinity uses to call us.
They are beautiful and wide ranging. They call us to be better, to do better, to love our neighbor as ourselves.

There is nothing to lose and much to gain.
Within this journey lies the potential for an Infinitude of everyday miracles.

The View From Within

In 1969, Joseph was graduating Stratford High School and I was just entering my freshman year there. We were each known to the other as we had a common bond- we were both performing artists in rock, rhythm and blues bands. After High school, Joseph's career took him on tour on the east coast and mine took me west to California. Throughout the years, we kept apprised of our travels and careers through friends and musicians of our mutual acquaintances.

In 2018 we reconnected. We spent hours getting to know each other again and had many long conversations catching up on our travels, love lives, families, and pursuits. I had become a wellness and happiness professor and he a photographer. While authoring a trilogy on happiness and after one of those crazy creative conversations, he offered to show me photographs of sacred places he had encountered in his world travels to see if they would be useful.
What a blessing!
The collaboration for this book began that day.

In order to encompass as many beautiful spiritual practices as we could, we began to travel the tri-state area together interviewing people of all faiths and traditions. This has been a beautiful experience. We have learned many things that we have shared in this book and we have opened our hearts to everyone we encountered.
Joe and I do not claim to be theologians or experts on any religion or denomination.

We are two seekers on the path. We experienced great joy making new friends and found that kindness and love greeted us in every interview.
The Spirit was always generously present.
This existential travel has given us an openness, a vibrancy,
and happiness we hope to share.

Donna holds a Master's degree in Counseling and Organizational Human Resource Development. She is a graduate of the Positive Psychology Program (the Science of Happiness) at Kripalu/ Wholebeing institute, and has worked as a teacher's assistant to WholeBeing Institute with Tal Ben Shahar, a renowned Harvard Professor author and authority on the science of Happiness.
Donna is a "Let Your Yoga Dance" Teacher. Trained by Nancy Megha Buttenheim at Kripalu

Donna is also post Master's certified in Positive Psychology Coaching, Teaching for Transformation, Mindfulness and Strength based practices through U PENN, VIA and Wholebeing Institute. She has additional certification in Women's Wellness and Meditation from Deepak Chopra, Wayne Dyer and UCLA.

Donna has an adjunct professorship at the University of Bridgeport where she teaches Wellness, Perspectives of Happiness and Human Services related courses.
Donna held The Executive Director position for 30 years at HELP FOR KIDS a positive parenting, family-strengthening Center in Southern Connecticut. She is an author, an international Key Note speaker, trainer and a presenter at National Conferences.
Donna is owner of "Happily Ever Actions" a business that helps people to live their best life now and that applies cutting-edge research to use the tenants of positive psychology in creating concrete tools that will increase happiness and well-being in all areas of life.
She is an expert in positive parenting education but will be the first to tell you that everything she has learned was from her wonderful children and grandchildren! She loves to sing the blues whenever she can and is currently co—authoring a series of books with her team of professionals working together towards
Happily Ever Actions ™ www.happilyeveractions.com
MS Donna Martire Miller MA, CIPP

Joseph Bologna became interested in photography watching his father take pictures of the family and developing them himself at home. He purchased his first camera in 1964 when he was 13. His thought was to photograph life extensively in order to "freeze time". He was also an avid reader and very creative.

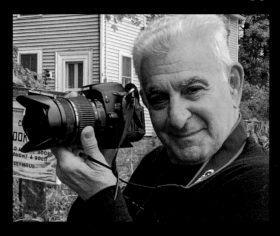

As he grew into his teens, he discovered that he had two things that really piqued his interest, reading about world-wide travel and music. He honed his photography skills while embarking on a career as a rock and roll performing artist. He captured the events as he toured the country with name acts. His love of photography became more aesthetic when he became a father in the 80's. He embraced a new system of image making that captured a more intimate portrait that was very detail oriented.

He became an event photographer for the schools, the Housatonic Counsel in CT, for weddings, portraits and the like. In 2005 he began his travels around the world as a photographer. His first trip was to Acapulco Mexico; his photography needed to be precise. He was meticulous in his approach to this art form. He would learn the lay of the land, the people's interests, their cultural norms and etiquette. Joseph began to love the people he would meet. He would find that the stresses of everyday life would disappear as he engaged in the photo shoots and captured the spirit of those he would meet along the way.

To date he has visited 26 countries around the world and has taken over 90,000 photos. He had a gallery on National Geographic. His work can be seen in travel magazines, private companies and businesses. In 2013 he was an instructor and held private photography classes. He has been peer awarded over 9,000 times and is considered a top 10 popular photographer in View Bug and has held that position since his enrollment as a member in 2016 to the present. He won the summer of 2020 people's choice award, the 2020 top shot and elite award. He is currently collaborating on a 3-book series featuring selected photographs and original writings as well as a series of children's books.

Notes: